Perfect Inventions=Perfect World

An **A**wesome **B**odacious **C**ool Book of Inventions
for the New Millennium

Perfect Inventions=Perfect World

An Awesome Bodacious Cool Book of Inventions for the New Millennium

Written and illustrated by the fifth-grade students of
Holly Springs Elementary School in Pickens, South Carolina

SCHOLASTIC INC.
New York   Toronto   London   Auckland   Sydney
Mexico City   New Delhi   Hong Kong

Go to www.scholastic.com for Web site information on Scholastic authors and illustrators.

Copyright © 2000 by Scholastic Inc.
All rights reserved. Published by Scholastic Inc.
SCHOLASTIC and associated logos
are trademarks and/or registered trademarks of Scholastic Inc.

ISBN 0-439-26066-3

12 11 10 9 8 7 6 5 4 3   01 02 03 04 05
                                                                                          23
Printed in the U.S.A.
First printing, October 2000

Introduction

In the last millennium, our world saw many new inventions and innovations. Advances in technology, along with other improvements, made our world a better place to live. Unfortunately, some of these inventions resulted in disaster and filled our world with violence, anger, pollution, and sadness.

Our inventions for the new millennium will correct these mistakes. As the next generation of leaders, scientists, and inventors, our actions will determine what kind of place the world will become. We will make life easier with machines and technology, but we will also protect our planet and fill the world with peace, love, and happiness.

Anticarcinomamort

A

anti
against (Greek)

carcinoma
cancer (Greek)

mort
death (Latin)

The Anticarcinomamort is an invention that cures cancer. When people are diagnosed with cancer and get their prescription filled, they request a certain flavor. Pharmacists create a powder from that flavor, add the secret ingredient, and turn it into pill form. With this invention, no one will ever have to suffer from cancer again.

Bellterra

bell
beautiful (Latin)

terra
Earth (Latin)

Bellterra makes the Earth a healthier and more beautiful place to live. It shoots out fertilizer and flower seeds and, at the same time, an invisible shield to catch pollution. There is so much pollution today, this invention would help our Earth recover from the damage we have done.

Culinchronoabbreviat

culin
kitchen (Latin)

chrono
time (Greek)

abbreviat
shortened
(Latin)

Culinchronoabbreviat is a robot that cooks and cleans. It can cook a full meal for your family in half the time it would take you to prepare it. This invention would be especially helpful for the sick and elderly.

Debilaeolgressor

debil
disabled, weak
(Latin)

aeol
quick-moving
(Greek)

gressor
walk (Latin)

The Debilaeolgressor is a vehicle that drives itself and will take you anywhere you want to go. It has a portable table and basket for your needs. It has a convertible roof and windshield wipers, and it runs on solar and lunar power. This is an invention that will help those who are handicapped to maneuver more easily.

E Ecdemaquarati

The Ecdemaquarati is an invention that can save people from drowning in vehicles. If your vehicle runs off a bridge, you land on floats that will keep your vehicle above the water until help arrives. Upon impact with water, a signal is sent to emergency rescue, and help is dispatched immediately. This invention will decrease the number of people who drown when their vehicle runs off a bridge.

Feniseccrambcotin

fenisec
mower (Latin)

cramb
cabbage (Latin)

cotin
wild olives
(Greek)

Feniseccrambcotin is an invention that harvests crops for farmers. It collects the crops and stores them in a big, temperature-controlled container to keep them fresh. It drives itself, so the farmer is free to do something else. It runs on fuel, but doesn't pollute. This invention will make hard-working farmers' lives a little easier.

Geoudegymnmiasm

geo
earth (Greek)

ude
ground (Greek)

gymn
bare (Greek)

miasm
pollution
(Greek)

The Geoudegymnmiasm makes litter a thing of the past. You plant the seed, add water, and the special plant grows. Its pollen spreads across a 100-mile radius, disintegrating any trash in that area. This invention is safe for plants and animals, does not aggravate allergies, and comes with a money-back guarantee!

H

hail
balls of ice
(Modern
English)

poma
cover (Greek)

The Hailpoma is an umbrella that is completely hail-safe. This umbrella is aluminum, but it folds up just like a regular one. This invention will secure the safety of people's heads during hailstorms.

Itezeuxi

ite
fossil
(Middle English)

zeuxi
joining (Greek)

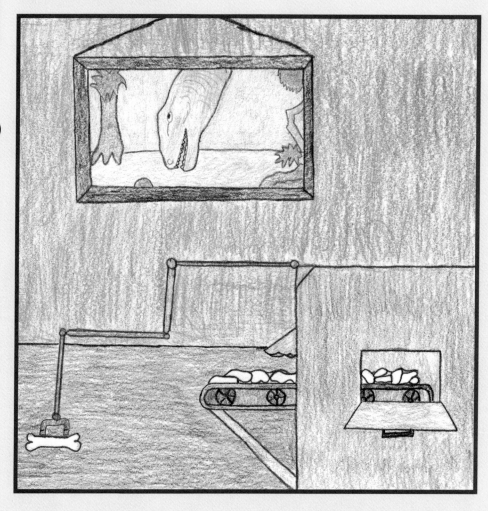

Itezeuxi is a machine that will help paleontologists reconstruct dinosaurs from fossilized bones. When you put the bones inside it, the robot arms construct the dinosaur into its original skeletal form. This invention will make it easier to put a dinosaur's bones together quickly, and free the paleontologist to search for more clues to our past.

Jejunlesticosus

jejun
hunger (Latin)

lest
rob (Latin)

icosus
ability (Greek)

Jejunlesticosus is an apparatus that sends food anywhere in the world. From a central control unit, food is sent in pods through pipes to every continent on Earth and is available to anyone who is hungry. This invention will insure that no one ever goes hungry again.

K Kaleidochoreopus

kaleido
beautiful form (Greek)

choreo
dance (Greek)

pus
foot (Greek)

Kaleidochoreopus are shoes that allow you to do any variety of dance in the world. A cord goes from your toe guard to the computer. You program your dance and unplug the shoes. When you tap the shoes together, the dance begins. This invention will not only help people who know how to dance, but also the people who now only dream about bringing this joy into their lives.

Lignyotlibera

lignyot
smoke (Latin)

libera
free (Latin)

Lignyotlibera assists people with a smoking problem. You just call the smoke-free hotline. The smoking antidote arrives in five minutes or less. If it doesn't get there in five minutes, it's free. This invention will help people quit smoking forever.

Multizoodromo

multi
many (Latin)

zoo
animals (Greek)

dromo
run (Greek)

The Multizoodromo helps animals get across the road safely. It is a bridge that covers the road. The animals walk on this bridge so they won't get run over. This invention will reduce the number of animals killed on our highways by 99.9% (especially possums!).

Nullivill

nulli
none (Latin)

vill
shaggy hair
(Latin)

Nullivill is a spray. It is like hairspray, but it doesn't harden. You spray it on your hair, and it fixes it so it won't stick up. Each can features a different hairstyle and is sold separately in stores near you. This will finally put an end to bad hair days.

NOTE: This product is safe for the ozone!

Ostracumsapor

ostracum
shell (Greek)

sapor
flavor (Latin)

Ostracumsapor is an ice-cream topping that cures ice-cream headaches. You decide which flavor you want and put it on your ice cream. It forms a yummy shell that makes ice-cream headaches a thing of the past.

Puroaquaantlia

puro
pure (Latin)

aqua
water (Latin)

antlia
pump (Latin)

Puroaquaantlia purifies water in rivers and lakes. Dirty water is sucked into the machine and goes through a cleaning cycle. Then it is released through pipes back into the lake or river. Today our rivers and lakes are polluted by factories, sewers, and litterbugs. This invention would purify them so all our water would be sparkling clean.

Questusthyrsapo

questus
complaint
(Latin)

thyr
shield (Greek)

sapo
soap (Latin)

Questusthyrsapo is a bar of soap that will make people stop complaining. Each time you wash, use Questusthyrsapo and your complaints will vanish. We need this soap so the complaining will stop in the new millennium.

Remedimishexis

R

remedi
cure (Latin)

mis
wrong (English)

hexis
habit (Greek)

The Remedimishexis is a pill that will stop people from becoming addicted to drugs and alcohol. All they need to do is take one pill every day for six months. This invention will forever eliminate all the problems and heartaches caused by alcohol and drug abuse.

S Sagolucrpilus

sago
a covering
(Greek)

lucr
gain (Latin)

pilus
hair (Latin)

The Sagolucrpilus is a hair-gaining cap that runs on solar power. It gives you hair when you are bald, and you can choose your hair color and your hairstyle. We need this machine because people are losing their hair at an alarming rate and their heads are freezing in winter.

Termtrapel

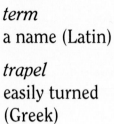

The Termtrapel is a microphone that you put on your tongue. As you are speaking one language, it translates your words into whatever language you want to speak. This invention will help people improve their communication skills all across the world.

Unklept

un
not (Latin)

klept
thief (Greek)

Unklept is a little camera placed in homes and stores. When a thief is leaving the building, the camera can see his or her face—even through a mask! It takes a picture of the thief's face, and the police look it up on a special computer to find the right suspect. This is a very good thing because people need to respect each other's property.

Virgautoperidin

V

virg
rod (Latin)

auto
self (Greek)

peridin
whirled about
(Greek)

The Virgautoperidin is a rod and reel that casts for you. You just push a button, and it automatically casts your hook where the fish are. It is designed to make the casting part of fishing easier, making fishing even more fun!

W Winterpachnpagus

winter
the coldest
season (English)

pachn
white (Greek)

pagus
ice, frost
(Greek)

The Winterpachnpagus is a Doppler radar system that notifies everyone when a blizzard or snowstorm is definitely coming. It also tells you how much accumulation you will get. This invention will prevent weathermen from getting kids' hopes up about incoming snow and school closings!

Xiphopax

xipho
sword (Greek)

pax
peace (Latin)

Xiphopax is a sword of peace. Every country has one. Whenever any government representative holds this sword, peace will come over the country. While in the past swords have been used to kill, this sword will save lives. Finally, there will be peace all over the world.

Y Yperinfelicarbor

Yperinfelicarbor is a tree that gives out air that makes people happy. During the process of photosynthesis, the tree not only puts out oxygen, it also puts out "happiness air." That way, every person in the world will be happy, not sad or scared.

Zorohabrovenus

Z

zoro
strong (Greek)

habro
delicate (Greek)

venus
goddess of love
and beauty
(Latin)

Zorohabrovenus is a bracelet (for girls) and a chain (for boys). This product fills people with love, replacing all the hate and prejudice. This product will help the world get through the new millennium with love.

Kids Are Authors®

Books written by children for children

The Kids Are Authors® Competition was established in 1986 to encourage children to read and to become involved in the creative process of writing. Since then, thousands of children have written and illustrated books as participants in the Kids Are Authors® Competition. The winning books in the annual competition are published by Scholastic Inc. and are distributed by Scholastic Book Fairs throughout the United States.

For more information:
Kids Are Authors®
Scholastic Book Fairs
PO Box 958411
Lake Mary, FL 32795-8411

Or visit our Web site at
www.scholasticbookfairs.com